Contents

The
SNOWMAN'S
Cold

Written and Illustrated by Gavin Bishop

"Sniff, sniff, sniff,"
went the snowman.
"I'm getting a cold."

"Ah-choo, ah-choo,"
sneezed the snowman.
"I'm getting the flu."

The snowman
sneezed and sneezed.
The snowman
coughed and wheezed.

The wind came by.
"I'll blow the clouds away,"
it said.
"Then the sun
can warm you up."

The sun shone down
and warmed up
the snowman.

Soon the snowman's
cold had gone...

and so had the snowman!

Storm

With one eye blue
and one eye brown,
Storm is the fastest
dog in town.

Through sleet and snow,
with careful tread,
he loves to run
and pull the sled.

"Mush!" calls the driver.
Go, Storm, go!
See him racing
through the snow.

Giselle Dawson

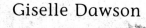

The SKI BUNNIES

Written by Louise Armstrong • Illustrated by Kelvin Hawley

It is race day
on the bunny slope.

The bunnies come with their skis.

They come
with their poles
and their goggles.

The bunnies hop
on the lift.
They go up, up, up.

"This is fun," they shout.
"But how do we get off?"

"Keep your ski tips up
and ski off,"
shouts the lift dog.

17

The ski bunnies line up
at the start of the race.

When the green flag
goes down, they take off
down the hill.

Some of the ski bunnies ski well.

Some of the ski bunnies fall in the snow.

What a race! Who will win?

19

Look at number ten.
Is he going to fall?

Yes!

No!

Number ten
wins first place.
Number ten
wins the ski bunny race!

Arctic fox

Polar bear

Walrus

Caribou

Lynx

Snowshoe hare

Red fox

Snowy owl

Leopard seal

Harp seal

22

Animals of the Ice and Snow

Arctic region

Antarctica

KEY

Killer whale

Humpback whale

King penguins

⊘ Arctic animals

⊘ Antarctic animals

Elephant seals

Albatross

23

Emperor Penguins

Written by Josh Ryan

Shake and Shiver

Emperor penguins live in Antarctica.
It is very cold in Antarctica.
The penguins huddle
in big groups
to keep warm.

Antarctica

Chick Chat

Emperor penguins
have their babies in winter.

The mother penguin lays an egg.
The father penguin
keeps the egg warm.

The father penguin
looks after the egg
for two months.
He doesn't eat at all.

After two months, a chick hatches.
The mother and father penguin
look after the chick.
The chick sits on their feet
to keep warm.

Growing Up

When the chick gets bigger, the mother and father penguin hunt for food in the sea. They take food to the chick.

Chicks stay together to keep warm.

Each chick
knows its
parent's call.

Waddle, Hop, Bellyflop

When the chicks are
five months old,
they go to the edge of the ice.
They jump into the sea.
They find their own food.

Penguins slide along
the ice and snow
on their bellies.

31

Fast Food

Emperor penguins eat
fish, shrimp, and crabs.
They can swim fast.
They can dive deep.
They can leap up onto the ice
to get away from killer whales.

Emperor penguins
are the biggest
penguins of all.
They can grow
as tall as a
seven-year-old
boy or girl.

1.2   4

1.0
       3

       2

       1

       0

m   ft

The Snowball Fight

Written by Pauline Cartwright * Illustrated by Andrea Jaretzki

Here comes a cloud,

quietly, quietly.

Here comes
the snow,
softly, softly.

Here comes
the night,
shivery,

shivery.

35

Here comes
the morning,
sparkly,
sparkly.

Here comes
my friend,
smiley,
smiley.

Here comes a snowball,
splattery, splattery.

Here comes
a **SNOWBALL FIGHT!**

GETTING READY FOR WINTER

> Which pictures belong together?

> How do the animals get ready for winter?

39

The Ants and the Grasshoppers

A Traditional Tale * Illustrated by Rebecca Allcock

It was summer.
The ants were busy
getting food for winter.

The grasshoppers were not busy.
They were playing
and singing in the grass.

41

All summer,
the ants were busy
getting food for winter.

All summer,
the grasshoppers played
and sang songs.

44

What lesson
do you think the ants
taught the grasshoppers?

Mountain Dogs
to the Rescue!

Every year, many people
are lost in the mountains
or buried in the snow.
Mountain dogs come to the rescue
with their good sense of smell.

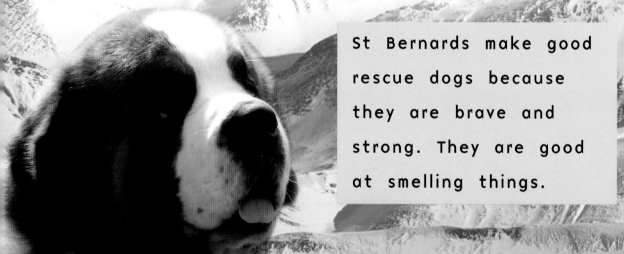

St Bernards make good
rescue dogs because
they are brave and
strong. They are good
at smelling things.

Alpine News • Monday, January 15

Brave Barry Does It Again!

Barry, the famous mountain-rescue dog, has saved the lives of two girls trapped high in the Swiss Alps.

Barry, the most famous St Bernard in Switzerland, in action in the snow.

Marie and her sister, Anna, slipped down a bank and were nearly buried in the snow.

"We would have been stuck there all night if it wasn't for Barry," said Anna later.

When the girls were late home from school, Barry and his master, Johann, were called to the rescue.

Using his keen sense of smell, Barry soon found the girls and quickly dug them out.

Barry has worked as a rescue dog for the last ten years. During this time, he has saved the lives of 40 people.

Snowflakes

Feathery flakes of snow
come down,
swirling, twirling, drifting,

until they cover
all the town,
swirling, twirling, drifting.

50

People hurry
to and fro,
riding, *sliding*, skipping,

through the *silvery*
powdered snow,
riding, *sliding*, skipping.

Louise Abney

51

Letters That Go Together

 gr   sk   sn

Sounds I Know

 -ee sneezed, wheezed

-ow blow, snow

Endings I Know

 **-ing** riding, sliding

-ly quietly, softly

Words I Know

all	it's	shouted	were
getting	keep	some	what
I'll	played	their	why
I'm	playing	them	with